CIVIL WAR ARTIST

Taylor Morrison

HOUGHTON MIFFLIN COMPANY BOSTON

For my brother, Daven

Thank you to David, Tom, and Jan for their patient and generous advice over the years. Thank you to Stan Nelson, David Paenco, Dr. Ana Lou Ashby, and Bridget Burke for their expert assistance with my research.

www.houghtonmifflinbooks.com

Library of Congress Cataloging-in-Publication Data
Morrison, Taylor.
   Civil war artist / written & illustrated by Taylor Morrison.
   p. cm.
   SUMMARY: Traces an illustrator's sketch of a Civil War battle from the time it leaves his hands, through the engraving and printing processes, and to its final publication in a newspaper.
   RNF ISBN 0-395-91426-4   PA ISBN 0-618-49538-X
   1. United States—History—Civil War, 1861–1865—Press coverage—Juvenile Literature.   2. United States—History—Civil War, 1861–1865—Journalists—Juvenile Literature.
3. Illustrators—United States—History—19th century—Juvenile Literature.   [1. United States—History—Civil War, 1861–1865—Press coverage.   2. Journalism.   3. Illustrators.]   I. Title.
   E468.9 .M86 1999
   070.4'499737—ddc21   97-52738
                                                      CIP
                                                      AC

ISBN-13: 978-0-618-49538-2

Printed in the United States of America
WOZ 10 9 8 7 6 5 4 3 2

4500422637

Imagine waiting four weeks to see pictures of the latest news. That was how long it took for readers of illustrated newspapers during the American Civil War. In 1861, when the war started, the papers hired artists to quickly sketch images of the fighting. These specialists risked their lives documenting battle scenes with only a sketchbook and pencils.

William Forbes and *Burton's Illustrated News* are fictitious, but they are closely based on the many long-forgotten sketch artists and illustrated newspapers. The huge teams of artists and newspaper workers of the 1800s devised new ways of delivering images to the American public. They also left us a clear and dramatic glimpse into the past.

In the summer of 1861, William Forbes came to New York City to make a living as an artist. He was unable to find work until he saw an important announcement in *Burton's Illustrated News*. It read: "Artists will be paid handsomely for sketches of the great battle between the Union and the Confederacy." William immediately joined a corps of artists that the newspaper was sending south by train. As the steam locomotive churned across the countryside, he anxiously double-checked his supplies: sketchbook, pencils, china white paint, blanket roll, canteen, bowie knife, revolver, war pass. William had to wait a few weeks in Washington, D.C., until the Union army moved west into Virginia. He then followed the thousands of marching soldiers.

A parade of people tagged along behind the army: newspaper reporters, sketch artists, spectators, and a photographer named Mathew Brady. During delays in the march, Brady would take pictures with his big bulky camera. Although his photographs were crystal clear, they could not capture movement, nor could they be printed in the newspapers of that time. It was left to the sketch artists to document the action of the coming battle.

On the morning of July 21, near a small creek called Bull Run, the opposing armies prepared for combat. Soon peaceful farmland was transformed into a terrifying battlefield. Great roars and flashes erupted from the artillery, sending deadly shells whistling through the air.

With only his pencil and paper, William tried to capture the gunners and officers rapidly firing and reloading their guns. He struggled to concentrate as stray bullets whizzed by his head and shells burst all around him.

He sketched the battle
in the heat and smoke.
He found it difficult to show
the fast-moving combat
accurately. All afternoon,
waves of Union and Rebel
troops fought back and forth
to win control of the field.

Late in the day the exhausted Union troops began to run off the battlefield in a chaotic retreat. Behind them charged a mob of Confederate soldiers. William watched in terror as the sun glinted off their sharp bayonets. He jumped on his horse and narrowly escaped.

That night William worked on a large drawing of the Battle of Bull Run. He looked over several rough sketches he had dashed off that day and tried to remember as much as he could about the battle. When the drawing was finished, he wrote down a few notes to help the newspaper's engravers re-create the complex scene. Early the next morning William gave the sketch to a courier. After several days of hard riding, the sketch was delivered to the busy offices of *Burton's Illustrated News.*

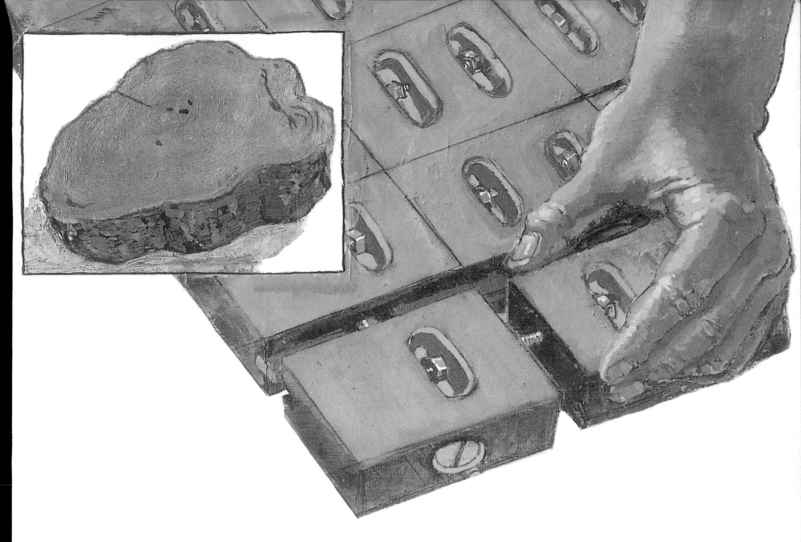

Down the street from *Burton's*, wood blocks were prepared in a wood-type factory. These blocks would be used to create a wood engraving from William's sketch. The best wood was fine-grained Turkish boxwood. Logs from this small tree were imported to America, sawed up, and placed in drying racks for two years. When the rounds dried out, pieces were cut from them that had no surface cracks or blemishes on their end grain. Small grooves were cut into the backs of the small blocks, and thirty-six of them were connected with tiny nuts and bolts. The resulting composite block provided a surface large enough for the engraving. The big block was then scraped and sandpapered until it was extremely smooth.

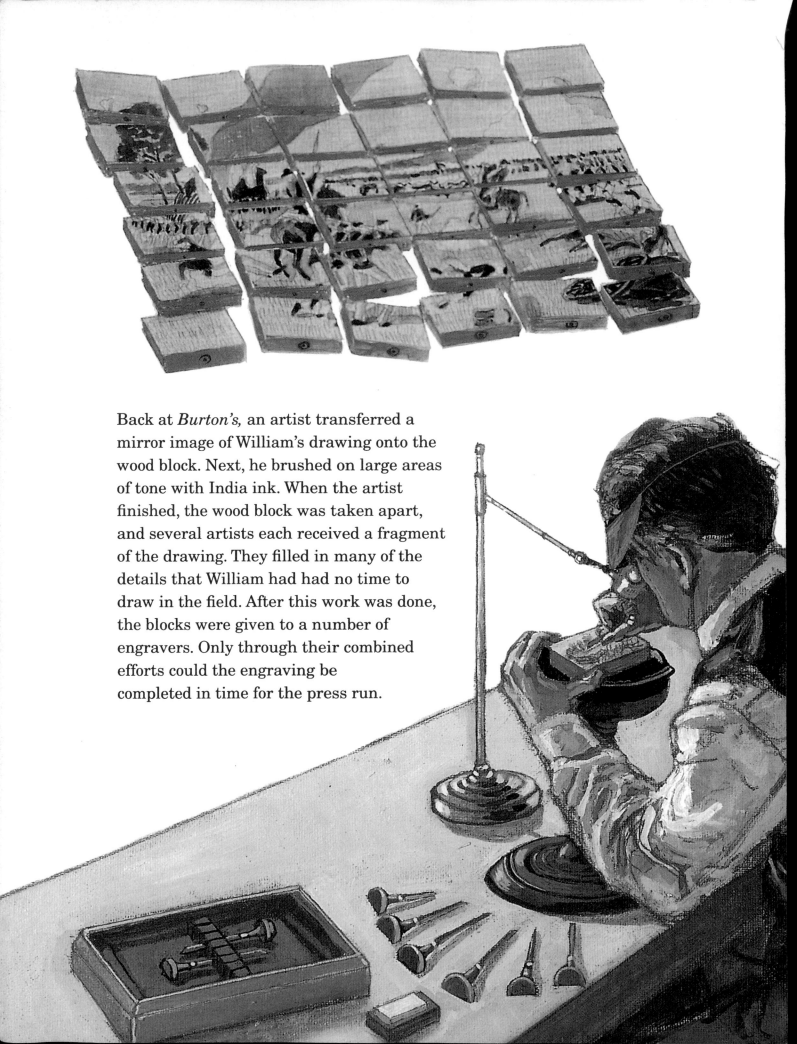

Back at *Burton's,* an artist transferred a mirror image of William's drawing onto the wood block. Next, he brushed on large areas of tone with India ink. When the artist finished, the wood block was taken apart, and several artists each received a fragment of the drawing. They filled in many of the details that William had had no time to draw in the field. After this work was done, the blocks were given to a number of engravers. Only through their combined efforts could the engraving be completed in time for the press run.

Each engraver had his specialty—trees, soldiers, artillery, horses, or background. With sharp steel gravers they cut out the white areas around the drawing and left the raised areas that would print black. The engravers also left a thin blank edge around each of their blocks. When all the blocks were

bolted together again, the master engraver had to complete the lines to connect the blocks. After working around the clock, the team of artists and engravers was finally finished with the huge engraving, which would be in the two-page centerfold of the newspaper.

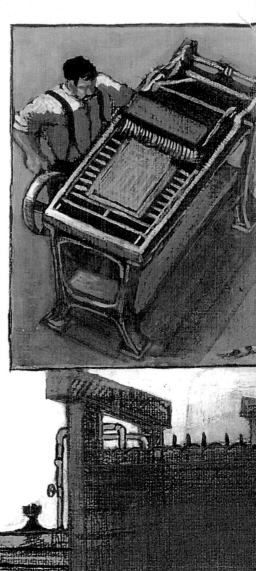

The ceaseless pounding of the printing press would break down an engraving, so it was preserved by electrotyping. The electrotyper placed a sheet of beeswax over the engraving in a powerful press. The wax was pressed into the engraving to create a perfect mold. Next, black lead was brushed onto the mold so that it would conduct electricity. The mold was then connected to the positive pole of a battery, a copper plate was connected to the negative pole, and both were dipped into a long tank full of copper sulphate. Electric current from the battery caused the copper plate to release tiny particles that were attracted to the mold. After ten hours the mold was lifted out of the tank coated with a thin shell of copper. The wax was melted off the back of the shell, molten lead was ladled in for a strong backing, and this backing was planed even. The electrotype was attached to a wooden base, making it the same height as printing type. Now it was ready for the press.

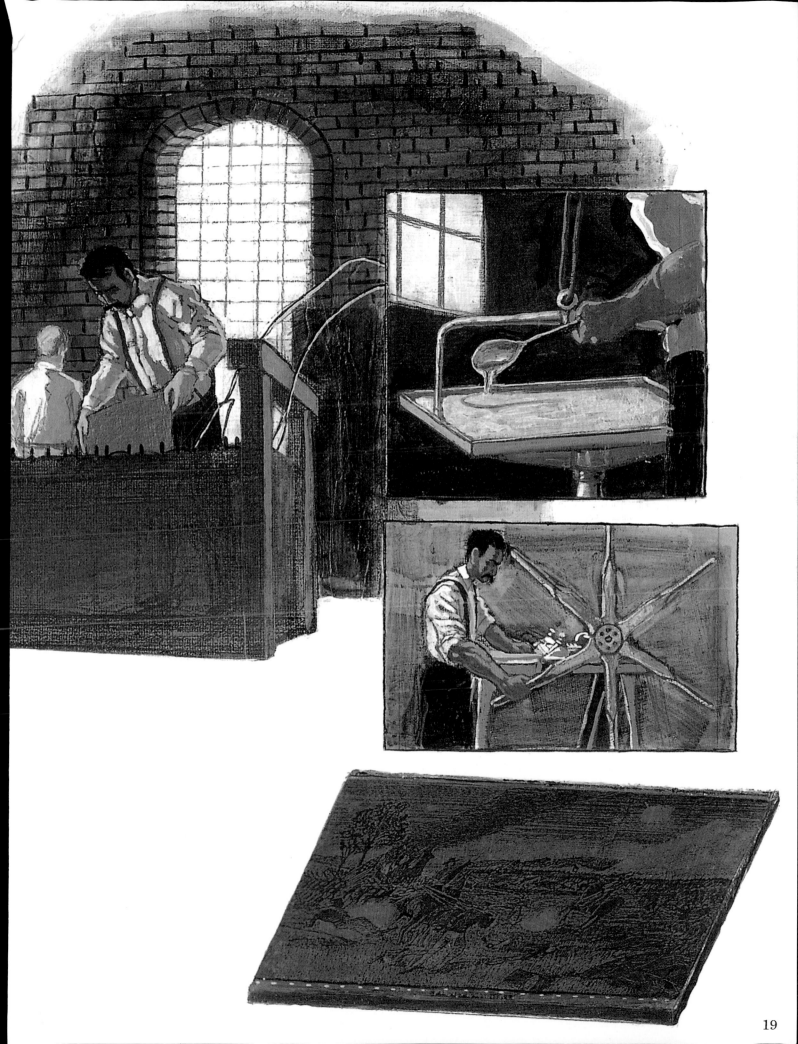

The electrotype and two other pages of the newspaper were locked into a heavy iron frame called a chase. The chase was then secured to the bed of a cylinder press. Another chase containing electrotyped engravings and text type was placed next to it. The bed of the press would print eight pages at a time, or half of the sixteen-page newspaper. The operator carefully checked over every inch of the plates to ensure that they would print properly. Then with a cry, "All ready!" a pressman pushed the long lever to start the press. Below, a massive steam engine powered the line running along the ceiling that set the massive cylinders in motion. Soon the room was filled with heat, the flapping of belts, and a steady hum of spinning wheels and gears.

A feeder stood at the top of the press and fed sheets of paper onto the revolving cylinder. The sheets were grabbed by small mechanical fingers, pulled under the big cylinder, pressed against the ink-covered type bed as it moved back and forth, and flung off by a big wooden comb called a fly.

Another pressman laid the sheets down and, because the paper was wet, he took the heavy piles of paper away before too many sheets built up. Every hour, the big press printed one thousand sheets. After both sides of the sheets were printed, they were folded, cut, and stacked for distribution.

On the morning of August 21, a crowd of eager newsboys gathered at the door of *Burton's* publication office. After fighting for the first supply of papers, they all ran off with their arms full. The boys roamed the streets of New York shouting out, "'Ere is *Burton's Illustrated News!* Get your noospaper!" Thousands of Americans gazed at William's dramatic picture of the Battle of Bull Run, four weeks after it happened.

Back in camp in Virginia, a mob of excited soldiers ran after the news train. A shower of papers flew off as it roared by. William was proud to see his drawing and impressed with the masterly work of the engravers.

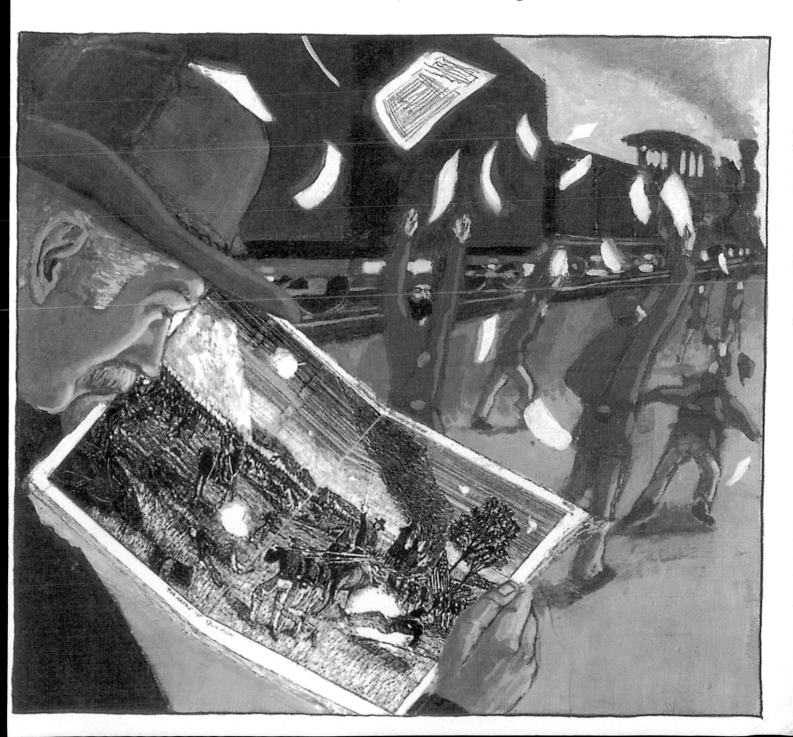

The war dragged on longer than anyone had expected. William continued to follow the Union army on its campaigns. He camped with the soldiers and shared their fear and hunger. Over the years he strove to send *Burton's* the best possible sketches. He often perched high in treetops or on top of earthworks, leaving the safety of cover for a better view. He kept on drawing for hours at a time while the bullets of Confederate sharpshooters whizzed by him. He rode through foul weather in pursuit of a sketch, and hoped that his paper would stay dry. After many exhausting days of sketching, he would stay up all night to finish a drawing by the dim flickering light of a campfire.

In 1864 William documented the great siege of Petersburg, Virginia. After nine months of brutal fighting, the exhausted Rebels evacuated the city. They surrendered in the small town of Appomattox on April 9, 1865. The Civil War, and William's days of reporting it, were finally over.

William continued to work as a sketch artist for *Burton's,* reporting on different stories up north. He often missed those dramatic days of the war, and made several paintings based on his sketches and memories.

In 1898 U.S. troops went off to Cuba to fight in the Spanish-American War. By this time William had retired, and he watched this war from his home rather than the battlefield. The pictures in the papers were different from those of the Civil War. The large, beautiful wood engravings had almost entirely vanished. A new and faster method of reproducing images called photoengraving had replaced the wood engravers' work. Now the pages were full of reproductions of oil paintings and photographs. William noticed a few blurry photographs capturing the action of the war. Photography and printing have come a long way since the Civil War, he thought. After the Spanish-American War, the papers began to hire photographers instead of illustrators. William was saddened to see the team of the sketch artist and the wood engraver disappear. Yet he often lifted his spirits by wondering what incredible ways people might see the news in the future.

GLOSSARY

Appomattox A small town in Virginia where the Confederate general Robert E. Lee surrendered to Ulysses S. Grant, ending the Civil War.

Artillery Large mounted guns or cannons.

Battle of Bull Run The first major land battle of the Civil War, where the Confederates soundly beat the Union.

Chase A rectangular metal frame that type and engravings are locked into for electrotyping or printing.

Chinese white An opaque white paint used by sketch artists to add highlights to their drawings on gray paper.

Confederacy (Rebels) A separate government of 11 southern states, which seceded from the Union in 1861.

Copper sulphate A chemical used to etch a copper plate in a tank during electrotyping.

Cylinder press A printing press consisting of a flat bed of printable material that passes under inking rollers and a big cylinder which presses paper against it.

Electrotyping A process that creates a durable metal printing plate from a mold made from lead type or wood engravings.

Engraver A highly skilled artist who made wood engravings for newspapers.

Fly A large wooden comb on cylinder presses that lifted printed sheets of paper off the press.

Gravers Sharp steel tools with different blades to make a wide variety of cut marks.

Line shafting Long shafts running along the ceiling that were attached to belts that powered printing presses.

Mathew Brady The most famous photographer of the Civil War.

Photoengraving A process using light and acid to etch an image into a metal printing plate. Photoengraving replaced the manual work of wood engraving late in the 19th century.

Siege of Petersburg A nine-month-long battle wherein Union forces attacked the town of Petersburg, which was an important railroad center for the Confederates.

Spanish-American War A short war in 1898 between the United States and Spain over the liberation of Cuba.

Steam engine Engines that ran nearly all of the machinery in businesses and factories during the 19th century.

Type bed A flat area on a cylinder press where the electrotyped plates are placed.

Type height The standard height of printing type and engravings, 0.918 inch.

Union The United States, 1861–1865, as it fought to keep its 34 states united during the Civil War.

Turkish boxwood An extremely fine grained and dense wood that is excellent for engraving. It was used often in the 19th century.

War pass Passes issued by the U.S. Army that allowed sketch artists to travel freely.

Wood type factory Factories that produced large wood type for posters and wood blocks for engravings.